British Warships
& Auxiliaries

(1983/4 Edition)

by Mike Critchley

HMS Swiftsure

£2.50

RFA Tidespring

INTRODUCTION

By Admiral Sir John Fieldhouse GCB, GBE First Sea Lord

It is a great pleasure for me to be asked to write the foreword for the 1983/4 edition of "British Warships and Auxiliaries". This compact but comprehensive publication has now established itself among the maritime publications of the country. It provides an excellent guide to the ships and aircraft of the Royal Navy and its supporting auxiliaries.

The flexible use of sea power has been of vital importance to our island nation throughout our history, and during the last year events in the South Atlantic have served, once again, as a reminder of the lessons of the past. It is incontrovertible that the operation mounted to regain possession of the Falkland Islands, with all the problems of distance, weather and logistic support that it involved, could not have been mounted otherwise than as a sea based campaign. It was essential that the Task Force should contain a balance of modern ships, including submarines and minesweepers. In addition it cannot be emphasised too strongly the role which was played by the Merchant Navy. Indeed, without the services of the Ships Taken Up From Trade, which ranged from the Queen Elizabeth II through tankers, support ships and cargo carriers to ocean going tugs, the operation could not have been mounted. How efficiently and effectively all these ships, Royal Navy, Royal Fleet Auxiliaries and Merchant Navy performed is well known and well documented so I will not repeat examples of their exploits here, but I would like to take this opportunity of reminding those of you who are sufficiently interested in the sea to be reading this book, of the complimentary and interlocking roles performed by such a variety of maritime power. For the United Kingdom to survive as an island and maritime nation it is essential that this balance, through the whole spectrum of sea power, is maintained.

We live in an age of rapid change, both in ship design and more particularly in weapon systems design, and it is therefore particularly credible that the author and publishers of this book manage to keep so well up to date and produce a comprehensive and accurate book every year. I can thoroughly recommend it to everyone who has an interest in the nations lifeline—the sea.

First Sea Lord.

THE ROYAL NAVY

If 1981 was the year of "The" Defence Review when, many long term plans for the future of the Royal Navy were given a severe jolt—1982 has undoubtedly had a similar effect on the Navy, thanks to events in the South Atlantic.

Whilst not attempting to distract in any way from the fact that victory was ours at the end of the day, there is no doubt that the whole operation has taught us plenty of lessons—some new, but many that should have been learned years ago.

No one involved in the campaign would disagree that, despite the best forces, equipment and planning, there were definite periods when the whole operation could have swung in the Argentinians favour. On more than one occasion luck was on our side.

Perhaps we should be grateful to the Argentinian Junta for deciding to annex the Falklands when they did. As it happened we were able to dispatch a task force. Many of the ships in it had, on paper, already made their last voyage. The ability to sail ships such as Fearless, Intrepid, Stromness and Tidepool was extremely fortunate to say the least. The fact that neither of our 'carriers was in major refit was a considerable factor in our ability to assemble the Force. Let there be no doubt that the mere ability to assemble and equip such a force in such a short time scale was one of the major successes of the whole operation. A great credit to the backroom boys, planners and the great British ability to improvise . . .

Many committees will doubtless meet for many hours to discuss the long term future of the Royal Navy after the Falklands. It is to be hoped that it will not be forgotten that the Navy's role is that of a Nato partner and the Falklands Conflict should, hopefully, be seen as a "one off" situation.

Is it beyond hope that we could put the "Great" back into Britain again and give our Navy back its historic role of international peace keepers? There can be no better time for the Royal Navy to be seen in strength throughout the world. The cost would be considerable of course but, as the Soviets have proved, where the flag goes, trade and influence follows . . . and that, these days seems to be what it is all about.

There can be little doubt that our Forces and their equipment are held in a new light overseas—the bulldog still has teeth and can bite—even if the politicians have made a few premature extractions! Now must be the time to wave the flag again—and for our arms salesmen to get to work with their now well tested products. Despite the protestations from some sectors of our society, let there be no doubt whatsoever that if overseas governments do not buy from us, there are plenty of other countries only too willing to supply military hardware—to whoever comes along. We live in a hard competitive world—and have paid dearly in the past for being "English gentlemen" overseas.

The Surface Fleet
Obviously the shape and size of the Feet is not going to change dramatically for the next few years—it will take more than the Falklands Campaign to change that. What has come over loud and clear from the ships returning from the South Atlantic is that for too long now our ships have been designed for comfort—not for conflict. Ship designers over recent years have produced a ship that looks a highly attractive "home from home" in the recruiting advert-

isements with plush formica bulkheads, foam mattresses and plastic fittings. It was these very items that caused so much damage in the South Atlantic, as shattered formica sliced through human limbs and burning mattresses and plastic fittings produced lethal smoke—within seconds of a ship being hit. Many "old timers" will recall that they had no such luxuries—and were spared the consequences of having them onboard. The space taken up by these modern living conditions is space that really should be allocated to weapon systems. A look at any modern warship of the Soviet navy will indicate the priorities they afford to the hardware. Living conditions for our conventional submariners—and our troops on the streets of Northern Ireland—are basic to say the least. Why the rest of our servicemen cannot have good but basic accommodation is unclear. Recruiting is not a problem—if conditions afloat are "too tough" for anyone they are surely those of whom the Services are best rid.

The future shape of the Navy of the nineties is now being decided. Money of course will always be a deciding factor—but as has been said many times before, if you want the insurance you have to pay the premium.

In coming years we will see a continuing reduction in the number of surface vessels in the fleet as the politicians plans for a much smaller Navy are implicated.

As the teeth of the Navy are once again being reduced, this year also sees the reductions in civilian support areas—as Chatham Dockyard heads for final closure and Portsmouth reduces. Despite these planned reductions, there are still areas where the cost cutting axe could well fall—a painful process for those employed in these areas but their loss could well be of benefit to the long term well being of the Fleet. The many MoD departments at Bath have escaped the axe in recent years, but it is rapidly approaching the time when the plug must be pulled! Many are an expensive luxury that can no longer be afforded in 1983. The huge MoD procurement executive is also an area that could easily be considerably reduced—many would hardly notice their demise.

Whilst on the subject of dockyards—only time will tell if the Fleet can operate efficiently with reduced dockyard capacity. Even before these reductions are implicated it is becoming clear that the Navy is having great difficulty refitting its nuclear hunter killer submarines to schedule. These highly complicated vessels always seem to be delayed once in dockyard hands—and the ability of Devonport and Rosyth Dockyard to cope with future work is an area of concern for senior officers. They would prefer to have these capital ships of today's Navy at sea—where they belong. They have no role to play in harbour.

Conventional Submarines
There still is no sign of an order for a replacement conventional submarine. Delays have occurred in trying to redesign the type 2400 so that it will suit potential overseas customers too. Hopefully these are now problems of the past. Even if orders were placed now it is going to be a considerable time before these boats appear in the Fleet—it is not intended that they are built at the rate of more than one per year.

Major Surface Units
The sale of INVINCIBLE to Australia having been cancelled in 1982 gives the Fleet the ability to have two of the class operational at one time (once Ark Royal is delivered)—whether Australia can be persuaded to order a new replacement remains to be seen. With elections in that country none too far away, it is going to need a very confident government to order such an expensive vessel. Even if the ship was ordered the type of aircraft she would carry is another expensive decision that needs to be taken.

The future of HERMES remains unclear, but manpower considerations alone will probably mean she will be sold overseas once the third Invincible is commissioned.

The Falklands Crisis has doubtless given a longer lease of life to the two assault ships, but they are expensive and awkward ships to maintain, and a decision must be taken shortly if they are to be replaced before the 1990s. Their role within Nato for the re-inforcement of Norway in times of tension, is considered vital and it may be that Nato money could be earmarked for their replacement. The retention of these ships has been a major shot in the arm for the Royal Marines, who were in real danger of losing most of their amphibious capability.

Escorts
Luckily the Navy has had some spare capacity, in the shape of the Standby Squadron, to replace ships lost in the South Atlantic. No doubt these somewhat older ships will be required for a few years yet for the many operational commitments the Fleet has. It will be a matter of years before any new escorts are available. It does seem odd that millions of pounds will be spent refitting already old ships such as Argonaut, Plymouth and Glamorgan, very badly mauled in the South Atlantic. Surely work-starved British shipbuilders could well have been given an order for a new vessel—albeit to an older design— than complete these "political" refits of the war veterans. Their age, if nothing else, will mean they will be scrapped in the near future, however much is spent on their current refits.

When an eventual "new frigate" does materialise, hopefully it will have overcome some of the problems of "non standardisation" within the Nato fleet. One has to be realistic, however, and conclude that it is most unlikely that we will be able to sell these ships to our Nato partners (national shipbuilders would not wear it) but there would appear to be considerable scope for sales to other Navies who have large amounts of ancient tonnage to replace within the next decade. Price and subsidies will of course sway decisions at the end of the day.

Minor Warships
With an announcement at last made for a new class of minecountermeasures vessels (for the RNR) there is hope that more orders will follow. Minecounter measurers has long been a Cinderella service. Things are slowly changing at last. Even if we are able to fight a future war—with our Nato partners—in the North Atlantic, there seems little point if our commercial ports are all closed, thanks to a handful of well placed mines. The rest of Europe can feed itself at least—but our ability to do so is doubtful. We are far more reliant on seaborne food supplies (and raw materials) than most people care to recollect. It cannot be said loud enough—and long enough, that our sadly depleted force of mine clearance vessels needs a major injection of new ships. Unlike the days of World War Two we cannot rely on a "lash-up" force of converted merchant ships. The modern mine is far too sophisticated and the stocks of such weapons held by the Soviets is huge.

Training Ships
The decision to remove Royal Marine detachments from frigates has released a number of billets for trainees in ships, but there is still a requirement for training afloat—how this will be accomplished is yet to be revealed.

Survey Ships
A large proportion of the survey programme was abandoned last year as the "Survey Navy" tackled its new task off the Falklands. Consequently a number of commercial hydrographic ships have been operating under MoD supervision to catch up on the backlog of work. As a large proportion of this work is carried out for other government departments, it will be interesting to see how the future of the hydrographic branch develops. There can be little doubt that commercial ships under contract can do the work at a considerably cheaper price.

If the MoD is not paying that bill the whole future of a large proportion of the Fleet could well be under threat from the Treasury. Standards, of course, are another matter.

Experimental Vessels

With no mention of hovercraft and Hydrofoils in this year's edition, it is clear that all the new experimental designs for warships of tomorrow have suffered the financial chop—an understandable move in hard times. It would seem a great pity that the Hovercraft—a British invention from the start—is now only in service in overseas Navies. It did appear that trials for service use for these craft were never ending—so the final whistle from the Treasury was perhaps long overdue.

The Fleet Air Arm

With most of the Fleet Air Arm having been deployed to the South Atlantic much combat experience has been gained—and hopefully established the Sea Harrier as a future export success. More replacements for the Sea Harriers lost will be slow in arriving, which will leave the number of these aircraft available for front line and training duties extremely small.

Probably the largest gap in available hardware in the South Atlantic was any form of airborne early warning radar. The Gannet, having been quietly allowed to disappear, with the demise of Ark Royal, could have played a vital role in the South Atlantic Conflict, had it been available.

There is now an urgent requirement to give the Fleet its "radar eyes" again. Already Sea Kings have been rapidly converted to carry a powerful radar aloft. A long term solution will doubtless come in the form of a converted commercial aircraft which can operate from an Invincible class ship. It would also make a lot of sense for this aircraft to have a dual capability. Electronic countermeasures (the Argentinians were surprisingly skilled at the art) need to be available with any Fleet. To have them available in a shorebased squadron of (RAF) aircraft is not good enough. These aircraft should be capable of embarking and operating from any suitable ship. There may even be a role for an airship in this increasingly essential area of modern warfare.

It is extremely easy to sit back and be an "armchair admiral" over these matters. We live in a country of ever increasing demands on a seemingly decreasing source of national revenue. Expenditure can only be allocated to yet more defence expenditure if the nation demands it—and the Services can be seen to cut waste to a minimum in both manpower and resources. With the recent announcement that over £60 million is spent annually on boarding school fees for servicemens' families, it is obvious that there are still plenty of places for money to be allocated to the "sharp end". Admittedly the civilian sector must take the brunt of these changes—but there is still plenty of scope for saving substantial amounts of money amongst uniformed members of the Service. Perhaps more financial clout should be given to Servicemen to put their own house in order rather than have them convince endless civilian review teams that their own individual small "empire" is vital.

SHIPS OF THE ROYAL NAVY — PENNANT NUMBERS

Ship	Penn. No.	Ship	Penn. No.
Aircraft Carriers		JUNO	F52
INVINCIBLE	R05	ARGONAUT	F56
ILLUSTRIOUS	R06	ANDROMEDA	F57
ARK ROYAL	R09	HERMIONE	F58
HERMES	R12	JUPITER	F60
		APOLLO	F70
Destroyers		SCYLLA	F71
KENT	D12	ARIADNE	F72
ANTRIM	D18	CHARYBDIS	F75
GLAMORGAN	D19	BROADSWORD	F88
FIFE	D20	BATTLEAXE	F89
BRISTOL	D23	BRILLIANT	F90
BIRMINGHAM	D86	BRAZEN	F91
NEWCASTLE	D87	BOXER	F92
GLASGOW	D88	BEAVER	F93
EXETER	D89	BRAVE	F94
SOUTHAMPTON	D90	YARMOUTH	F101
NOTTINGHAM	D91	LOWESTOFT	F103
LIVERPOOL	D92	DIDO	F104
MANCHESTER	D95	ROTHESAY	F107
GLOUCESTER	D96	LONDONDERRY	F108
EDINBURGH	D97	LEANDER	F109
YORK	D98	FALMOUTH	F113
CARDIFF	D108	AJAX	F114
		BERWICK	F115
Frigates		ESKIMO	F119
AURORA	F10	GURKHA	F122
ACHILLES	F12	ZULU	F124
EURYALUS	F15	PLYMOUTH	F126
DIOMEDE	F16	PENELOPE	F127
GALATEA	F18	RHYL	F129
CLEOPATRA	F28	NUBIAN	F131
ARETHUSA	F38	TARTAR	F133
NAIAD	F39	AMAZON	F169
SIRIUS	F40	ACTIVE	F171
PHOEBE	F42	AMBUSCADE	F172
TORQUAY	F43	ARROW	F173
MINERVA	F45	ALACRITY	F174
DANAE	F47	AVENGER	F185

Ship	Penn. No.	Ship	Penn. No.
Submarines		**Minesweepers &**	
SEALION	SO7	**Minehunters**	
WALRUS	SO8	ST DAVID	M07
OBERON	SO9	VENTURER	M08
ODIN	S10	BRECON	M29
ORPHEUS	S11	LEDBURY	M30
OLYMPUS	S12	CATTISTOCK	M31
OSIRIS	Si3	COTTESMORE	M32
ONSLAUGHT	S14	BROCKLESBY	M33
OTTER	S15	MIDDLETON	M34
ORACLE	S16	DULVERTON	M35
OCELOT	S17	CHIDDINGFORD	M36
OTUS	S18	HURWORTH	M37
OPOSSUM	S19	ALFRISTON	M1103
OPPORTUNE	S20	BICKINGTON	M1109
ONYX	S21	BILDESTON	M1110
RESOLUTION	S22	BRERETON	M1113
REPULSE	S23	BRINTON	M1114
RENOWN	S26	BRONINGTON	M1115
REVENGE	S27	WILTON	M1116
CHURCHILL	S46	CRICHTON	M1124
CONQUEROR	S48	CUXTON	M1125
COURAGEOUS	S50	BOSSINGTON	M1133
VALIANT	S102	GAVINTON	M1140
WARSPITE	S103	HODGESTON	M1146
SCEPTRE	S104	HUBBERSTON	M1147
SPARTAN	S105	IVESTON	M1151
SPLENDID	S106	KEDLESTON	M1153
TRAFALGAR	S107	KELLINGTON	M1154
SOVEREIGN	S108	KIRKLISTON	M1157
SUPERB	S109	LALESTON	M1158
SWIFTSURE	S126	MAXTON	M1165
		NURTON	M1166
		POLLINGTON	M1173
		SHAVINGTON	M1180
Assault Ships		SHERATON	M1181
FEARLESS	L10	UPTON	M1187
INTREPID	L11	WALKERTON	M1188
		WOTTON	M1195
		SOBERTON	M1200

Ship	Penn. No.	Ship	Penn. No.
STUBBINGTON	M1204	**Survey Ships & RN**	
LEWISTON	M1208	**Manned Auxiliaries**	
CROFTON	M1216	BRITANNIA	A00
		ECHO	A70
Patrol Craft		ENTERPRISE	A71
PEACOCK	P239	EGERIA	A72
PLOVER	P240	MANLEY	A92
STARLING	P241	MENTOR	A94
SWALLOW	P242	MILLBROOK	A97
SWIFT	P243	MESSINA	A107
ALERT	P252	HECLA	A133
VIGILANT	P254	HECATE	A137
LEEDS CASTLE	P258	HERALD	A138
KINGFISHER	P260	HYDRA	A144
CYGNET	P261	ENDURANCE	A171
PETEREL	P262	WAKEFUL	A236
SANDPIPER	P263	BULLDOG	A317
DUMBARTON		IXWORTH	A318
CASTLE	P265	BEAGLE	A319
ANGLESEY	P277	FOX	A320
ALDERNEY	P278	FAWN	A335
JERSEY	P295	WATERWITCH	M2720
GUERNSEY	P297	WOODLARK	M2780
SHETLAND	P298	CHALLENGER	K07
ORKNEY	P299		
LINDISFARNE	P300		
BEACHAMPTON	P1007		
MONKTON	P1055		
WASPERTON	P1089		
WOLVERTON	P1093		
YARNTON	P1096		
DROXFORD	P3113		

KEEP RIGHT UP TO DATE

The 1984 edition of this book will be available in Nov 1983.

If you wish to be informed when it is available write to:—
Maritime Books, Duloe, Liskeard, Cornwall.

Ship	Penn. No.
Minelayer	
ABDIEL	N21

HMS Resolution

RESOLUTION CLASS

Ship	Pennant Number	Completion Date	Builder
RESOLUTION	S22	1967	Vickers
REPULSE	S23	1968	Vickers
RENOWN	S26	1968	C. Laird
REVENGE	S27	1969	C. Laird

Displacement 8,400 tons (submerged) **Dimensions** 130m x 10m x 9m **Speed** 25 knots **Armament** 16 Polaris Missiles, 6 Torpedo Tubes **Complement** 147 (x 2).

Notes

These four nuclear-powered Polaris submarines are the United Kingdom's contribution to NATO's strategic nuclear deterrent. At least one of them is constantly on partol and because of their high speed, long endurance underwater, and advanced sensor and electronic equipment they have little fear of detection.

Each submarine carries 16 Polaris two-stage ballistic missiles, powered by solid fuel rocket motors, 9.45 metres long, 1.37 metres diameter and weighing 12,700 kilogrammes. Fired from the submerged submarine it can devastate a target 2,500 nautical miles away.

HMS Courageous

VALIANT CLASS

Ship	Pennant Number	Completion Date	Builder
CHURCHILL	S46	1970	Vickers
CONQUEROR	S48	1971	C. Laird
COURAGEOUS	S50	1971	Vickers
VALIANT	S102	1966	Vickers
WARSPITE	S103	1967	Vickers

Displacement 4,900 tons dived **Dimensions** 87m x 10m x 8m
Speed 28 knots + **Armament** 6 Torpedo Tubes.
Complement 103

Notes

DREADNOUGHT—the forerunner of this class—is now awaiting disposal (by scrap or sinking) at Chatham. These boats are capable of high underwater speeds and can remain on patrol almost indefinitely. They are able to circumnavigate the world without surfacing.

HMS Splendid

SWIFTSURE CLASS

Ship	Pennant Number	Completion Date	Builder
SCEPTRE	S104	1978	Vickers
SPARTAN	S105	1979	Vickers
SPLENDID	S106	1980	Vickers
SOVEREIGN	S108	1974	Vickers
SUPERB	S109	1976	Vickers
SWIFTSURE	S126	1973	Vickers

Displacement 4,500 tons dived **Dimensions** 83m x 10m x 8m **Speed** 30 knots + dived **Armament** 5 Torpedo Tubes. **Complement** 116.

Notes

A follow-on class of ships from the successful Valiant Class. These submarines have an updated Sonar and Torpedo system and are the very latest in submarine design. A new class of updated Swiftsure Class are under construction. The first HMS TRAFALGAR was launched in 1981. HM Ships TURBULENT & TIRELESS and at least two others will follow.

HMS Sealion

PORPOISE CLASS

Ship	Pennant Number	Completion Date	Builder
SEALION	S07	1961	C. Laird
WALRUS	S08	1961	Scotts

Displacement 2,410 tons (submerged) **Dimensions** 90m x 8m x 5m **Speed** 12 knots surfaced, 17 submerged **Armament** 8 Torpedo Tubes **Complement** 70.

Notes
Diesel electric powered submarines that were the first submarines to be designed and built after the war. Capable of long underwater patrols, but mainly used for exercise and training purposes as more Nuclear submarines join the Fleet. The 1981 Defence review stated "We will proceed as fast as possible with a new and more effective class to replace our ageing diesel-powered submarines". This will be the Vickers Type 2400—now long awaited. Tenders have been invited but still no firm orders placed.

14

HMS Odin

OBERON CLASS

Ship	Pennant Number	Completion Date	Builder
OBERON	S09	1961	Chatham D'yard
ODIN	S10	1962	C. Laird
ORPHEUS	S11	1960	Vickers
OLYMPUS	S12	1962	Vickers
OSIRIS	S13	1964	Vickers
ONSLAUGHT	S14	1962	Chatham D'yard
OTTER	S15	1962	Scotts
ORACLE	S16	1963	C. Laird
OCELOT	S17	1964	Chatham D'yard
OTUS	S18	1963	Scotts
OPOSSUM	S19	1964	C. Laird
OPPORTUNE	S20	1964	Scotts
ONYX	S21	1967	C. Laird

Displacement 2,410 tons (submerged) **Dimensions** 90m x 8m x 5m **Speed** 12 knots surface, 17 knots submerged **Armament** 8 Torpedo Tubes **Complement** 70.

Notes

Very similar to Porpoise Class. Upper casing is made of glass fibre — the first time plastics have been used in submarine construction.

HMS Hermes

HERMES CLASS

Ship	Pennant Number	Completion Date	Builder
HERMES	R12	1959	Vickers

Displacement 28,700 tons **Dimensions** 229m x 27m x 9m
Speed 28 knots **Armament** 2 Sea Cat Missile Systems, 9 Sea
King helicopters, 5 Sea Harrier aircraft, 2 Wessex helicop-
ters **Complement** 980 + aircrews.

Notes
A former fixed wing aircraft carrier converted to a Commando
Carrier in 1971-73. Refitted in 1976 into an Anti-submarine
Carrier and again in 1981 (for Sea Harrier operations). Flagship
for the Falkland Islands Task Force. Due to be sold/scrapped
as a defence economy but future unclear. May be sold to India
or Australia.

HMS Illustrious

INVINCIBLE CLASS

Ship	Pennant Number	Completion Date	Builder
INVINCIBLE	RO5	1979	Vickers
ILLUSTRIOUS	RO6	1982	Swan-Hunter
ARK ROYAL	RO9		Swan-Hunter

Displacement 19,500 tons **Dimensions** 206m x 32m x 6.5m **Speed** 28 knots **Armament** Sea Dart Missile System **Aircraft:** 5 x Sea Harrier, 10 x Sea King **Complement** 900 + aircrews.

Notes

A new generation of mini-aircraft carriers long awaited by the Royal Navy to provide air cover for a task group of ships. A "ski-ramp" is fitted to enable the Sea Harrier a greater payload on take-off.

The sale of INVINCIBLE to Australia cancelled during Falklands conflict. When third ship is completed—two can be kept operational at any one time.

HMS Fearless

FEARLESS CLASS

Ship	Pennant Number	Completion Date	Builder
FEARLESS	L10	1965	Harland & Wolff
INTREPID	L11	1967	J. Brown

Displacement 12,500 tons, 19,500 (flooded) **Dimensions** 158m x 24m x 8m **Speed** 20 knots **Armament** 4 Sea Cat Missile Systems, 2 x 40mm guns **Complement** 580.

Notes

Multi-purpose ships that can operate helicopters for embarked Royal Marine Commandos. 4 landing craft are carried on an internal deck and are flooded out when ship docks down. One ship is usually in refit/reserve. The other is used to train young officers from the RN College, Dartmouth (currently FEARLESS), but still retains amphibious capabilities. Can embark 5 Wessex helicopters. Both ships were reprieved from the scrapman — and rapidly sailed with the Falkland Islands Task Force. INTREPID has now reverted to 'Standby' status.

A S S A U L T   S H I P S

HMS Bristol firing Ikara

BRISTOL CLASS (Type 82)

Ship	Pennant Number	Completion Date	Builder
BRISTOL	D23	1972	Swan Hunter

Displacement 6,750 tons **Dimensions** 154m x 17m x 7m **Speed** 30 knots + **Armament** 1 x 4.5″ gun, Ikara Anti-submarine Missile System, 1 Sea Dart Missile System, 2 x 20mm guns **Complement** 407.

Notes
Four ships of this class were ordered but three later cancelled when requirement for large escorts for fixed wing aircraft carriers ceased to exist. Helicopter Deck provided but no aircraft normally carried. Now used as a Flagship. Early retirement was planned but will now be retained in the active Fleet.

HMS Glamorgan

COUNTY CLASS

Ship	Pennant Number	Completion Date	Builder
KENT	D12	1963	Harland & Wolff
ANTRIM	D18	1970	Fairfield
GLAMORGAN	D19	1966	Vickers
FIFE	D20	1966	Fairfield

Displacement 6,200 tons **Dimensions** 159m x 16m x 6m, **Speed** 32 knots **Armament** 2 x 4.5″ guns, 2 x 20mm guns, 4 Exocet Missiles, 1 x Sea Slug Missile System. Seacat. **Complement** 485

Notes

KENT has 2 extra 4.5″ guns and no Exocet missile system. Each ship has a Wessex Mk 3 helicopter embarked but may re-equip with a Lynx helicopter. KENT is used as a Harbour Training Ship at Portsmouth (future uncertain after mid 1983). LONDON sold to Pakistan and NORFOLK to Chile in 1982.

HMS Liverpool

SHEFFIELD CLASS (Type 42)

Ship	Pennant Number	Completion Date	Builder
BIRMINGHAM	D86	1976	C. Laird
NEWCASTLE	D87	1978	Swan Hunter
GLASGOW	D88	1978	Swan Hunter
EXETER	D89	1980	Swan Hunter
SOUTHAMPTON	°D90	1981	Vosper T.
NOTTINGHAM	D91	1982	Vosper T.
LIVERPOOL	D92	1982	C. Laird
● MANCHESTER	D95	1983	Vickers
● GLOUCESTER	D96	Building	Vosper T.
● EDINBURGH	D97	Building	C. Laird
● YORK	D98	Building	Swan Hunter
CARDIFF	D108	1979	Vickers

Displacement 3,660 tons **Dimensions** 125m x 15m x 7m **Speed** 30 knots + **Armament** 1 x 4.5 " gun, 4 x 30mm guns, 4 x 20mm guns, Sea Dart Missile System: Lynx Helicopter. 6 Torpedo Tubes. **Complement** 280 + ● "stretched" Type 42.

Notes
Will not now undergo "mid-life" modernisation. Sister ships SHEFFIELD and COVENTRY sunk during Falklands conflict. Extra 20mm & 30mm guns fitted during, and after, Falklands crisis in place of ships boats.

HMS Battleaxe

BROADSWORD CLASS (Type 22)

Ship	Pennant Number	Completion Date	Builder
BROADSWORD	F88	1978	Yarrow
BATTLEAXE	F89	1980	Yarrow
BRILLIANT	F90	1981	Yarrow
BRAZEN	F91	1982	Yarrow
● BOXER	F92	Building	Yarrow
● BEAVER	F93	Building	Yarrow
● BRAVE		Building	Yarrow

Displacement 3,860 tons **Dimensions** 131m x 15m x 4m **Speed** 29 knots **Armament** 4 Exocet Missiles, 2 Sea Wolf Missile Systems, 2 x 40mm guns, 6 Torpedo Tubes, 2 Lynx helicopters **Complement** 224. ● "Stretched" Type 22.

Notes
Designed as eventual replacements for the Leander Class frigates. Two further ships have been ordered. More may be built.

HMS Andromeda

LEANDER CLASS

Ship	Pennant Number	Completion Date	Builder
ACHILLES	F12	1970	Yarrow
DIOMEDE	F16	1971	Yarrow
JUNO	F52	1967	Thornycroft
● ANDROMEDA	F57	1968	HM Dockyard Portsmouth
● HERMIONE	F58	1969	Stephen
● JUPITER	F60	1969	Yarrow
APOLLO	F70	1972	Yarrow
● SCYLLA	F71	1970	HM Dockyard Devonport
ARIADNE	F72	1972	Yarrow
● CHARYBDIS	F75	1969	Harland & Wolff

Displacement 2962 tons **Dimension** 113m x 13m x 5m **Speed** 27 knots **Armament** 2 x 4.5″ guns, 2 x 20mm guns, 1 Sea Cat Missile System, 1 Mortar Mk 10, 1 Wasp helicopter. **Complement** 260.

Only ships marked ● will now be converted to carry the Sea Wolf missile system. JUNO will eventually replace TORQUAY as a Training Ship. BACCHANTE sold to New Zealand 1982.

FRIGATES

23

HMS Naiad

LEANDER CLASS (Ikara Conversions)

Ship	Pennant Number	Completion Date	Builder
AURORA	F10	1964	J. Brown
EURYALUS	F15	1964	Scotts
GALATEA	F18	1964	S. Hunter
ARETHUSA	F38	1965	Whites
●NAIAD	F39	1965	Yarrow
DIDO	F104	1963	Yarrow
LEANDER	F109	1963	Harland & Wolff
AJAX	F114	1963	C. Laird

Displacement 2,860 tons **Dimensions** 113m x 12m x 5m
Speed 29 knots **Armament** 1 Ikara Anti Submarine Missile,
2 x 40mm guns, 2 Sea Cat Missile Systems, 1 Mortar Mk 10,
1 Wasp helicopter **Complement** 240.

Notes
All ships were converted (1973-76) to carry the Ikara Anti
submarine Missile System (forward of the bridge) in lieu of
a 4.5" gun. The Wasp helicopter is being replaced in all ships
by the Lynx. ● Earmarked for disposal (1982) but may now
remain in active or standby fleet.

HMS Penelope

LEANDER CLASS (Exocet Conversions)

Ship	Pennant Number	Completion Date	Builder
CLEOPATRA	F28	1966	HM Dockyard Devonport
SIRIUS	F40	1966	HM Dockyard Portsmouth
PHOEBE	F42	1966	Stephens
MINERVA	F45	1966	Vickers
DANAE	F47	1967	HM Dockyard Devonport
ARGONAUT	F56	1967	Hawthorn Leslie
PENELOPE	F127	1963	Vickers

Displacement 2,860 tons **Dimensions** 113m x 12m x 5m **Speed** 27 knots **Armament** 4 Exocet Missiles, 3 Sea Cat Missile Systems, 2 x 40mm guns, 6 Torpedo Tubes, 1 Lynx helicopter **Complement** 230.

Notes

The highly successful Leander Class are the last steam powered frigates in the Royal Navy, all later ships being propelled by gas turbines. PHOEBE now refitted with extra 20mm guns but no forward Seacat mounting.

HMS Arrow

AMAZON CLASS (Type 21)

Ship	Pennant Number	Completion Date	Builder
AMAZON	F169	1974	Vosper T.
ACTIVE	F171	1977	Vosper T.
AMBUSCADE	F172	1975	Yarrow
ARROW	F173	1976	Yarrow
ALACRITY	F174	1977	Yarrow
AVENGER	F185	1978	Yarrow

Displacement 3,250 tons **Dimensions** 117m x 13m x 6m **Speed** 34 knots **Armament** 1 x 4.5″ gun, 2 x 20mm guns, 4 Exocet Missiles, 1 Sea Cat Missile System, 1 Wasp/Lynx helicopter **Complement** 170.

Notes

Most of the class now have 6 torpedo tubes each.
These General Purpose frigates were built to a commercial design by Vosper/Yarrow and subsequently sold to the Ministry of Defence. Sister ships ANTELOPE and ARDENT sunk during Falklands conflict.

HMS Gurkha

TRIBAL CLASS (Type 81)

Ship	Pennant Number	Completion Date	Builder
● ESKIMO	F119	1963	White
GURKHA	F122	1963	Thornycroft
ZULU	F124	1964	Stephen
● NUBIAN	F131	1962	HM Dockyard Portsmouth
TARTAR	F133	1962	HM Dockyard Devonport

Displacement 2,700 tons **Dimensions** 110m x 13m x 5m **Speed** 28 knots **Armament** 2 x 4.5" guns, 2 x 20mm guns, 2 Sea Cat Missile Systems, 1 Mortar Mk 10, 1 Wasp helicopter **Complement** 250.

General Purpose Frigates built for service in the Middle East and West Indies. They were the first ships built to carry a helicopter and have combined steam and gas turbine propulsion. GURKHA, ZULU & TARTAR were in the Standby Squadron at Chatham, but were brought forward for service during the Falklands crisis. Their "life-span" in the active fleet is undecided. ● Approved to scrap.

ROTHESAY CLASS (Type 12)

Ship	Pennant Number	Completion Date	Builder
YARMOUTH	F101	1960	J. Brown
LOWESTOFT	F103	1961	Stephen
ROTHESAY	F107	1960	Yarrow
FALMOUTH	F113	1961	Swan Hunter
BERWICK	F115	1961	Harland & Wolff
PLYMOUTH	F126	1961	HM Dockyard Devonport
RHYL	F129	1960	HM Dockyard Portsmouth

Displacement 2,800 tons **Dimensions** 113m x 13m x 5m
Speed 30 knots **Armament** 2 x 4.5″ guns, 2 x 20mm guns, 1
Sea Cat Missile System, 1 Mortar Mk 10, 1 Wasp helicopter.
Complement 250.

Notes

All ships of this class were follow-on ships to the Whitby Class
and then converted to carry a helicopter.
RHYL, FALMOUTH & BERWICK were temporarily reprieved
from the scrap man by the Falklands crisis and, the last two
named, brought forward for service from the Standby Squadron
at Chatham. Their "reprieve" could be short lived.

HMS Torquay

TYPE 12 (Trials Ships)

Ship	Pennant Number	Completion Date	Builder
TORQUAY	F43	1956	Harland & Wolff
LONDONDERRY	F108	1960	J.S. White

Displacement 2,800 tons **Dimensions** 112m x 12m x 5m
Speed 29 knots **Armament** 2 x 4.5" guns, 1 Mortar Mk 10.
Complement 250.

Notes
TORQUAY is used as a Navigational Training Ship.
LONDONDERRY was extensively modernised to fit her for a
trials role. The ship's weapons systems were removed and
replaced by a computer and new communications and navi-
gation equipment. Although paid off early on a defence
economy LONDONDERRY was recommissioned as a training
ship once the Falklands crisis broke—and remains in service.

HMS Brocklesby

MINE COUNTERMEASURES SHIPS (MCMV's)
BRECON CLASS

Ship	Pennant Number	Builder
BRECON	M29	Vosper T.
LEDBURY	M30	Vosper T.
CATTISTOCK	M31	Vosper T.
COTTESMORE	M32	Yarrow
BROCKLESBY	M33	Vosper T.
MIDDLETON	M34	Yarrow
DULVERTON	M35	Vosper T.
CHIDDINGFORD	M36	Vosper T.
HURWORTH	M37	Vosper T.

Displacement 625 tonnes **Dimensions** 60m x 10m x 2.2m
Speed 17 knots **Armament** 1 x 40mm gun **Complement** 45.

Notes

A new class of MCMV being built, albeit in small numbers, to replace the ageing Coniston Class over the next few years. The largest Warships ever to be built in Glass Reinforced Plastic. First five in service—remainder building. More orders for the RN under consideration.

An expected sale to Australia has now been cancelled.

HMS St David

Ship	Pennant Number	Completion Date	Builder
ST DAVID	MO7	1972	Cubow
VENTURER	MO8	1973	Cubow

Displacement 392 tonnes **Dimensions** 36m x 9m x 4m
Speed 14 knots. Unarmed. **Complement** 35.

Notes
These two ships are commercial trawlers on charter to the Ministry of Defence. Formerly the Suffolk Harvester (ST DAVID) & Suffolk Monarch. They are equipped for deep team sweeping and operate together as a pair. Both are manned by the RNR.
An order for a new class of Minesweeper (now to be known as Fleet Minesweepers) has now been made. Four ships ordered will be for RNR. The first will be in service in 1983.

MCM VESSELS

HMS Cuxton

CONISTON CLASS

Ship	Pennant Number	Ship	Pennant Number
*ALFRISTON (S)	M1103	HUBBERSTON (H)	M1147
§BICKINGTON (S)	M1109	IVESTON (H)	M1151
BILDESTON (H)	M1110	*KEDLESTON (H)	M1153
*BRERETON (H)	M1113	*KELLINGTON (H)	M1154
BRINTON (H)	M1114	KIRKLISTON (H)	M1157
BRONINGTON (H)	M1115	*LALESTON (S)	M1158
WILTON (H)	M1116	MAXTON (H)	M1165
§CRICHTON (S)	M1124	NURTON (H)	M1166
§CUXTON (S)	M1125	§POLLINGTON (S)	M1173
BOSSINGTON (H)	M1133	§SHAVINGTON (S)	M1180
GAVINTON (H)	M1140	SHERATON (H)	M1181
*HODGESTON (S)	M1146	UPTON (S)	M1187

HMS Lewiston

CONISTON CLASS (Cont.)

Ship	Pennant Number	Ship	Pennant Number
§WALKERTON (S)	M1188	§STUBBINGTON(S)	M1204
§WOTTON (S)	M1195	*LEWISTON (S)	M1208
§SOBERTON (S)	M1200	*CROFTON (S)	M1216

Displacement 425 tons **Dimensions** 46m x 9m x 3m **Speed** 15 knots **Armament** 1 x 40mm gun, 2 x 20mm guns (removed in some ships) **Complement** 29/38

Notes

120 of this class were built in the early 50s but many have now been sold overseas or scrapped. Have fulfilled many roles over many years and have given excellent service. WILTON, built of glassfibre in 1974, was the world's first 'plastic' warship. Ships marked * are sea training tenders for the RNR. Ships marked § are employed on Coastal Fishery Protection duties. Ships marked (S) are Minesweepers — (H) Minehunters.

HMS Abdiel

MINELAYER
ABDIEL CLASS

Ship	Pennant Number	Completion Date	Builder
ABDIEL	N21	1967	Thornycroft

Displacement 1,500 tons **Dimensions** 80m x 13m x 4m **Speed** 16 knots **Armament** 44 mines 1 x 40mm **Complement** 77.

Notes

Designed as a Headquarters and Support Ship for mine counter measure forces and exercise minelayer. Workshops & spares embarked enable minecountermeasures ships to operate well away trom home bases.

ABDIEL is the only operational minelayer in the Royal Navy but plans exist to use merchant ships to lay mines if required.

HMS Dumbarton Castle

CASTLE CLASS (OPV2)

Ship	Pennant Number	Completion Date	Builder
LEEDS CASTLE	P258	1981	Hall Russell
DUMBARTON CASTLE	P265	1982	Hall Russell

Displacement 1450 tonnes **Dimensions** 81m x 11m x 3m
Speed 20 knots **Complement** 40 **Armament** 1 x 40mm gun

Notes

These ships have a dual role — that of fishery protection and offshore patrols within the limits of UK territorial waters — No less than 270,000 sq. miles! The OPV2 design is seen by the builders as a multi-purpose vessel with a primary role in off-shore protection but with the flexibility to operate as a missile-armed gunboat or anti-submarine corvette. Unlike the Island Class these ships are able to operate helicopters—including Sea King aircraft. Further orders are under consideration.

PATROL VESSELS

35

The Hong Kong Squadron

PATROL BOATS

Ship	Pennant Number	Completion Date	Builder
BEACHAMPTON	P1007	1953	Goole SB
MONKTON	P1055	1956	Herd Mackenzie
WASPERTON	P1089	1956	J.S. White
WOLVERTON	P1093	1957	Montrose SYCo.
YARNTON	P1096	1956	Pickersgill

Displacement 425 tons **Dimensions** 46m x 9m x 3m **Speed** 15 knots **Armament** 2 x 40mm guns **Complement** 32.

Notes

Former Coastal Minesweepers converted to Patrol Boats in 1971 for service in Hong Kong. Conversion involved removal of most minesweeping equipment and fitting extra 40mm gun aft of the funnel. All will gradually be retired as Peacock Class enter service.

HMS Lindisfarne

ISLAND CLASS

Ship	Pennant Number	Completion Date	Builder
ANGLESEY	P277	1979	Hall Russell
ALDERNEY	P278	1979	Hall Russell
JERSEY	P295	1976	Hall Russell
GUERNSEY	P297	1977	Hall Russell
SHETLAND	P298	1977	Hall Russell
ORKNEY	P299	1977	Hall Russell
LINDISFARNE	P300	1978	Hall Russell

Displacement 1,250 tons **Dimensions** 60m x 11m x 4m
Speed 17 knots **Armament** 1 x 40mm gun **Complement** 39.

Notes

Built on trawler lines these ships were introduced to protect the extensive British interests in North Sea oil installations and to patrol the 200 mile fishery limits.

Artists impression of HMS Peacock

PEACOCK CLASS

Ship	Pennant Number	Completion Date	Builder
PEACOCK	P239	1983	Hall Russell
PLOVER	P240	1983	Hall Russell
STARLING	P241	1984	Hall Russell
SWALLOW	P242	1984	Hall Russell
SWIFT	P243	1984	Hall Russell

Displacement 700 tons **Dimensions** 62m x 10m x 5m **Speed** 25 knots **Armament** 1 x 76mm gun **Complement** 44

Notes

These five new ships will replace the aging Ton class Patrol Vessels in Hong Kong waters over the next two years. They will be given the first RN warships to carry the 76mm Oto Melara gun. Considerably faster vessels than those they are to replace, they will be used to provide an ocean going back-up to the Marine Department of the Hong Kong Police. The Government of Hong Kong is paying 75% of the building and maintenance costs of these vessels.

HMS Droxford

SEAWARD DEFENCE BOAT

Ship	Pennant Number	Completion Date	Builder
DROXFORD	P3113	1954	Pimblott
Displacement 142 tons **Dimensions** 36m x 6m x 2m **Speed** 18 knots **Complement** 20.			

Notes

Sole survivor of a class designed and built to patrol and defend harbour approaches—equipped with depth charges. Remains in service as training ship for RN Unit at Glasgow University.

HMS Woodlark

TRAINING SHIPS

Ship	Pennant Number	Completion Date	Builder
WATERWITCH	M2720	1960	J.S. White
WOODLARK	M2780	1959	J.S. White

Displacement 160 tons **Dimensions** 32m x 7m x 2m **Speed** 12 knots **Complement** 19

Notes
Former Inshore Survey Craft now used as training ships for RN University units (WATERWITCH at Liverpool & WOOD-LARK at Southampton).

HMS Kingfisher

BIRD CLASS

Ship	Pennant Number	Completion Date	Builder
KINGFISHER	P260	1975	R. Dunston
CYGNET	P261	1976	R. Dunston
PETEREL	P262	1976	R. Dunston
SANDPIPER	P263	1977	R. Dunston

Displacement 190 tons **Dimensions** 37m x 7m x 2m **Speed** 21 knots **Armament** 1 x 40mm gun **Complement** 24

Notes

Based on the RAF long range recovery vessels, these craft were built for fishery protection duties. They have not been very successful as they have proved to be bad seaboats. PETEREL and SANDPIPER are now used by Britannia Royal Naval College, Dartmouth, as training ships — the other two ships are employed on coastal patrol duties.

HMS Manly

Ship	Pennant Number	Completion Date	Builder
MANLY	A92	1982	R. Dunston
MENTOR	A94	1982	R. Dunston
MILLBROOK	A97	1982	R. Dunston
MESSINA	A107	1982	R. Dunston

Displacement 150 tons **Dimensions** 25m x 6m x 3m **Speed** 10 knots **Armament** Nil **Complement** 13

Notes

Very similar to the RMAS/RNXS tenders. These four craft are all employed on training duties (first three named attached to HMS RALEIGH for new entry training). They have replaced Inshore Minesweepers used until 1982.

IXWORTH (A318) is similar. Ex RMAS she now flies the White Ensign.

HMS Hecate (note grey paintwork)

HECLA CLASS

HMS Herald

Ship	Pennant Number	Completion Date	Builder
HECLA	A133	1965	Yarrow
HECATE	A137	1965	Yarrow
HERALD	A138	1974	Robb Caledon
HYDRA	A144	1966	Yarrow

Displacement 2,733 **Dimensions** 79m x 15m x 5m **Speed** 14 knots **Complement** 115.

Notes

Able to operate for long periods away from shore support, these ships and the smaller ships of the Hydrographic Fleet collect the data that is required to produce the Admiralty Charts which are sold to mariners worldwide. Each ship usually carries a Wasp hellcopter. HERALD is an improved version of the earlier ships. HECATE armed (2 x 20mm) and painted grey in 1982 as a temporary replacement for ENDURANCE in the South Atlantic.

S
U
R
V
E
Y

S
H
I
P
S

HMS Bulldog

BULLDOG CLASS

Ship	Pennant Number	Completion Date	Builder
BULLDOG	A317	1968	Brooke Marine
BEAGLE	A319	1968	Brooke Marine
FOX	A320	1968	Brooke Marine
FAWN	A335	1968	Brooke Marine

Displacement 1,088 tons **Dimensions** 60m x 11m x 4m **Speed** 15 knots **Complement** 39.

Notes

Designed to operate in coastal waters. A new slightly larger survey ship is planned. It is being designed to enable operations in the more exposed continental shelf areas.

HMS Enterprise

INSHORE SURVEY CRAFT

Ship	Pennant Number	Completion Date	Builder
ECHO	A70	1958	J.S. White
ENTERPRISE	A71	1959	M.W. Blackmore
EGERIA	A72	1959	Wm. Weatherhead

Displacement 160 tons **Dimensions** 32m x 7m x 2m **Speed** 14 knots **Complement** 19.

Notes
Built for survey work in harbours and river estuaries. These craft are due to be paid off in 1984/85 and are planned to be replaced by a sidewall hovercraft and 15 metre launch.

HMS Endurance

ICE PATROL SHIP

Ship	Pennant Number	Completion Date	Builder
ENDURANCE (ex MV Anita Dan)	A171	1956	Krogerwerft Rendsburg

Displacement 3,600 tons **Dimensions** 93m x 14m x 5m
Speed 14 knots **Armament** 2 x 20mm guns **Complement** 124.

Notes

Purchased from Denmark in 1967 ENDURANCE is painted brilliant red for easy identification in the ice of Antarctica where she spends 6 months of the year. Her role is to undertake oceanographic and hydrographic surveys in the area and support scientists working ashore. A small Royal Marine detachment is embarked. Two Wasp helicopters are carried for rapid transport of personnel & stores. Was to have been "retired early" after her 1982 season in Antarctica, but reprieved as a result of the Falklands crisis.

HMY Britannia

ROYAL YACHT

Ship	Pennant Number	Completion Date	Builder
BRITANNIA	A00	1954	J. Brown

Displacement 4,961 tons **Dimensions** 126m x 17m x 5m
Speed 21 knots. **Complement** 270.

Notes
Probably the best known ship in the Royal Navy, BRITANNIA was designed to be converted to a hospital ship in time of war but this conversion was not made during the Falklands crisis. Is used for NATO exercises when not on 'Royal' business. Dark blue hull and buff funnel. Two extensive refits have brought the ship up to modern-day standards. Normally to be seen in Portsmouth Harbour when not away on official duties.

Two Pieces of History for Your Bookshelf . . .

FALKLANDS TASK FORCE PORTFOLIO

HM-SM Opportune

HMS Londonderry

F108

HMS Hermes

HMS Liverpool

HMS Guernsey

HMS Leeds Castle

HMS Britannia

RFA Resource

HMS Zulu

HMS Superb

HMS Wakeful

TUG/SUBMARINE TENDER

Ship	Pennant Number	Builder
WAKEFUL (Ex Dan)	A236	Cochranes
Displacement 900 tons **Dimensions** 44m x 11m x 5m **Speed** 14 knots **Complement** 25.		

Notes

Purchased from Swedish owners in 1974 for duties in the Clyde area as Submarine Target Ship and at the Clyde Submarine Base — HMS NEPTUNE. Has been used for Fishery Protection work and the shadowing of Soviet warships in British waters. Has proved very expensive to keep in service.

HMS Challenger—fitting out

SEABED OPERATIONS VESSEL

Ship	Pennant Number	Completion Date	Builder
CHALLENGER	K07	Building	Scott Lithgow

Displacement 6,400 tons **Dimensions** 134m x 18m x 5m **Speed** 15 knots **Complement** 185.

Notes

CHALLENGER will be equipped to find, inspect and, where appropriate, recover objects from the seabed at greater depths than is currently possible. She is designed with a saturation diving system enabling up to 12 men to live in comfort for long periods in a decompression chamber amidships, taking their turns to be lowered in a diving bell to work on the seabed. Also fitted to carry out salvage work. Until CHALLENGER is ready for service the MV SEAFORTH CLANSMAN (3,300 tons) is on charter to the MoD — and operates with an RN diving team.

BH7

HOVERCRAFT

The Royal Naval Hovercraft Trials Unit at Lee-on-Solent is equipped with the following Hovercraft:

    3 SRN 6 Craft — For Patrol duties. (2 now in Hong Kong)

    1 BH.7 Craft — Trials Craft and MCM support role.

    1 VT2 Craft — Support duties for Minecountermeasures forces.

THE
ROYAL FLEET AUXILIARY

The Royal Fleet Auxiliary service is operated by the Director of Fuel, Movements and Victualling whose directorate forms part of the Royal Navy Supply and Transport Service (RNSTS) within the Ministry of Defence (Navy). The RNSTS provides the total logistic support for the Royal Navy and is civilian manned throughout under the management of the Director General of Supplies and Transport (Navy).

All Royal Fleet Auxiliaries are manned by Merchant Navy personnel and operate under their own distinctive flag—a blue ensign with a vertical anchor in gold on the fly, which distinguishes them from the other non-commissioned ships and craft engaged in the Naval service. All officers and some 40-50% of ratings serve under contract to the Royal Fleet Auxiliary Service.

The RFA Fleet currently comprises 4 large fleet tankers (OL and Tide classes), 5 smaller fleet tankers (Rover class), 5 support tankers (Leaf class), 5 store support ships (one Ness class, Regent, Resource and two Fort class), RFA Engadine (helicopter support ship) and 4 landing ships (logisitic) supporting the British Army of the Rhine (Sir Lancelot class).

As a result of the government's commitment to reduce public expenditure the Royal Fleet Auxiliary Service, along with other Defence departments, has taken its share of the cuts. Until the Falklands crisis other cuts were to be expected in 1983. Only time will tell if these further reductions in the size of the Fleet are likely to be implemented

Whatever moves are made in the short term, the long term future of the service remains bright. The afloat support role of the service continues to grow placing new demands on its officers and ratings and calling for greater operational sophistication and flexibility.

The future will also see the advent of a newer and more versatile RFA—combining features which are now present in separate vessels all in one hull. The need for this type of vessel in the Fleet train has long been discussed and a firm commitment to build these new ships must be reached shortly if delivery is required before the end of the decade.

Although the primary role of the RFA service remains the underway replenishment of fuel, stores, ammunition and food to the Fleet, the frequent embarkation of Sea King helicopters in front line RFA's give many an anti-submarine training role in support of the Royal Navy. This role has added an extra dimension calling for new skills in seamanship and flight deck operations from RFA personnel.

With the increasing reliance of the Fleet on RFA support it is essential that the protection of these vessels is given greater priority. The Sea Kings embarked are more than able to offer anti-submarine protection. It remains to be seen, again as a result of the Falklands conflict, if some form of protection against air attack is fitted to these large ships. It may even be that, like some of our NATO partners, we may have to arm our auxiliaries and consequently man them with servicemen. The useful facility to operate these ships as "Merchant Ships" is one that will not be given up easily, but the day when this happens cannot be far away. The similarity between some RFA's and a more conventional Merchant Ship are sometimes hard to recognise.

Whilst the role played by the RFA during the Falklands crisis is well known and acknowledged, mention must be made of the ability of the Merchant Service to provide ships and manpower—at extremely short notice—for service in the South Atlantic. It was a remarkable achievement to provide this Merchant back-up force to the RFA.

If the Merchant Navy is allowed to reduce rapidly in size—as we have seen in recent years—the day may not be too far away when we would be unable to repeat the exercise.

SHIPS OF THE ROYAL FLEET AUXILIARY
Pennant Numbers

Ship	Penn. No.	Ship	Penn. No.
TIDESPRING	A75	STROMNESS	A344
PEARLEAF	A77	FORT GRANGE	A385
PLUMLEAF	A78	FORT AUSTIN	A386
APPLELEAF	A79	RESOURCE	A480
BRAMBLELEAF	A81	REGENT	A486
BAYLEAF	A109	ENGADINE	K08
OLWEN	A122	SIR BEDIVERE	L3004
OLNA	A123	SIR GERAINT	L3027
OLMEDA	A124	SIR LANCELOT	L3029
GREEN ROVER	A268	SIR PERCIVALE	L3036
GREY ROVER	A269	SIR TRISTRAM	L3505
BLUE ROVER	A270	(Hulk)	
GOLD ROVER	A271		
BLACK ROVER	A273		

RFA Olna

'OL' CLASS

Ship	Pennant Number	Completion Date	Builder
OLWEN	A122	1965	Hawthorn Leslie
OLNA	A123	1966	Hawthorn Leslie
OLMEDA	A124	1965	Swan Hunter

Displacement 36,000 tons **Dimensions** 197m x 26m x 10m **Speed** 19 knots **Complement** 94.

Notes

These ships can carry up to 3 Wessex helicopters. Dry stores can be carried — and transferred at sea — as well as a wide range of fuel, aviation spirit and lubricants. One ship may be placed in Reserve in 1983/84.

RFA Tidespring

TIDE CLASS

Ship	Pennant Number	Completion Date	Builder
TIDESPRING	A75	1963	Hawthorn Leslie

Displacement 27,400 tons **Dimensions** 177m x 22m x 10m
Speed 18 knots **Complement** 110.

Notes

Built to fuel warships at sea in any part of the world including strengthening for ice operations. A hangar and flight deck provides space for three Wessex helicoptors if required. Was due to be "retired early" during 1982/3. But reprieved for Falklands crisis. TIDEPOOL sold to Chile 1982.

RFA Gold Rover

ROVER CLASS

Ship	Pennant Number	Completion Date	Builder
GREEN ROVER	A268	1969	Swan Hunter
GREY ROVER	A269	1970	Swan Hunter
BLUE ROVER	A270	1970	Swan Hunter
GOLD ROVER	A271	1974	Swan Hunter
BLACK ROVER	A273	1974	Swan Hunter
Displacement 11,522 tons **Dimensions** 141m x 19m x 7m **Speed** 18 knots **Complement** 50.			

Notes
Small Fleet Tankers designed to supply HM ships with fresh water, dry cargo and refrigerated provisions as well as a range of fuel and lubricants. Due to initial engineering problems some of the class have had to be re-engined.

RFA Brambleleaf

LEAF CLASS [New]

Ship	Pennant Number	Completion Date	Builder
APPLELEAF	A79	1980	Cammell Laird
BRAMBLE-LEAF	A81	1980	Cammell Laird
BAYLEAF	A109	1982	Cammell Laird

Displacement 37,747 tonnes **Dimensions** 170m x 26m x 12m **Speed** 14.5 knots **Complement** 60.

Notes

APPLELEAF and BRAMBLELEAF are ex Merchant Vessels (Hudson Deep & Hudson Cavelier) taken over by the Ministry when part completed. BAYLEAF is a sister ship owned by Lombard North Central Ltd and on charter to MOD.

RFA Pearleaf

LEAF CLASS [Old]

Ship	Pennant Number	Completion Date	Builder
PEARLEAF	A77	1960	Blythwood
PLUMLEAF	A78	1960	Blyth D.D.

Displacement Both about 25,000 tons **Dimensions** 170m x 22m x 7m **Speed** 15 knots **Complement** 55.

Notes

These 2 different ships are on long term charter to the Ministry of Defence from their civilian owners and are employed on freighting duties between oil terminals, but have limited replenished facilities to fuel HM ships at sea. Both due to have been deleted from RFA Fleet but reprieved by Falklands crisis. Will now remain in service.

RFA Fort Grange

FORT CLASS

Ship	Pennant Number	Completion Date	Builder
FORT GRANGE	A385	1978	Scott Lithgow
FORT AUSTIN	A386	1979	Scott Lithgow

Displacement 17,000 tons **Dimensions** 183m x 24m x 9m
Speed 20 knots **Complement** 133.

Notes

These ships can carry a wide range of armament stores, ammunition, naval stores, dry and refrigerated provisions and NAAFI stores for supply to warships at sea.

Full hangar and maintenance facilities are provided and up to four Sea King helicopters can be carried for both the transfer of stores and anti-submarine protection of a group of ships.

RFA Stromness

NESS CLASS

Ship	Pennant Number	Completion Date	Builder
STROMNESS	A344	1967	Swan Hunter

Displacement 16,500 tons **Dimensions** 160m x 22m x 7m **Speed** 17 knots **Complement** 105.

Notes
Brought forward from Reserve for rapid deployment with Falklands Task Force. Sister ships now sold to US Navy. The future of this ship has yet to be decided.

STORES SHIPS

RFA Regent

REGENT CLASS

Ship	Pennant Number	Completion Date	Builder
RESOURCE	A480	1967	Scotts
REGENT	A486	1967	Harland & Wolff

Displacement 22,890 tons **Dimensions** 195m x 24m x 8m **Speed** 21 knots **Complement** 123.

Notes

The only RFA ships with an RN helicopter permanently embarked for supplying ships with a full range of the Naval Armament stores and ammunition carried aboard. A limited range of Naval Stores and food is also carried. RESOURCE may well be placed in Reserve or sold.

RFA Sir Bedivere

LANDING SHIPS
SIR LANCELOT CLASS

Ship	Pennant Number	Completion Date	Builder
SIR BEDIVERE	L3004	1967	Hawthorn
SIR GERAINT	L3027	1967	Stephen
SIR LANCELOT	L3029	1964	Fairfield
SIR PERCIVALE	L3036	1968	Hawthorn

Displacement 5,550 tons **Dimensions** 126m x 18m x 4m
Speed 17 knots **Armament** Can be fitted with 2 x 40mm guns
in emergency **Complement** 69.

Notes
Manned by the RFA but tasked by the Army, these ships are
used for heavy transport of stores — embarked by bow and
stern doors — and beach assault landings. Can operate helicopters from tank deck if required. SIR GALAHAD and SIR
TRISTRAM fatally struck during bombing raids in the Falklands conflict. SIR GALAHAD was later sunk as a war grave.
SIR TRISTRAM in temporary use as an accommodation hulk in
Port Stanley. Replacements are expected to be ordered.

RFA Engadine

RFA ENGADINE

Ship	Pennant Number	Completion Date	Builder
ENGADINE	K08	1967	Robb

Displacement 9,000 tons **Dimensions** 129m x 17m x 7m
Speed 16 knots **Complement** 73 (+ RN group).

Notes

Specially built for RFA service (but with embarked RN personnel) to provide training ship for helicopter crews operating in deep waters well away from coasts. Can operate up to 6 helicopters and often embarks pilotless target aircraft for exercises. Hangar for them above main hangar.

ROYAL MARITIME AUXILIARY SERVICE

The Royal Maritime Auxiliary Service Fleet, comprising 600 hulls, of which 380 are self propelled, is currently one of the largest marine undertakings in the country. It is administered by the Director of Marine Services (Naval) to whom the Captains of the Ports and Resident Naval Officers at the various Naval Bases are mainly responsible for the provision of Marine Services for the Royal Navy. They also supply many types of craft for the numerous and diverse requirements of other Ministry of Defence departments.

Ships of the RMAS, which can be seen at work in any of the Naval Bases throughout the United Kingdom and at Gibraltar, are easily identified by their black hulls and buff coloured superstructure and funnels, and by the RMAS flag, which is a blue ensign defaced in the fly by a yellow anchor over two wavy lines. The pennant numbers of the larger ships are painted in white on the black hulls.

The largest section of the fleet is employed on harbour duties, the types of vessels involved being Harbour Tugs, Fleet Tenders, Tank Cleaning Lighters, Harbour Launches, Naval Armament Vessels, and Dumb Lighters for carrying ammunition, general stores, oil, water and victuals to the Royal Navy, NATO Navies and Royal Fleet Auxiliary Ships when they are in port or at anchor.

A smaller section of the fleet, is, however, engaged in a purely sea-going capacity. Ocean Tugs, Torpedo Recovery Vessels, and Mooring and Salvage Vessels are designed and equipped for world wide towing and complex Marine Salvage operations. Experimental Trials Vessels, fitted with some of the most modern sophisticated equipment, are deployed on a wide range of duties in the fast growing area of advanced experimental technology necessary for the design of new ships, weapons and machinery.

Oil pollution is becoming more prevalent, and to deal with emergencies which may arise around the coastline of the United Kingdom, the RMAS has adapted many of its vessels to carry dispersant chemicals and to fit spraying equipment as a prerequisite to assisting the Department of Trade in combating oil pollution in waters outside Dockyard Ports.

In keeping with the overall policy of reducing the surface fleet, outlined in the 1981 Defence Review, the RMAS is being reduced in both manpower and vessels. With the closure of Chatham Naval Base and the run down at Portsmouth, many of the older units of the fleet will disappear without replacement, and new construction will make use of multi-role vessels. Before changes can be implemented, however, the needs of the users of the various types of RMAS vessels, e.g. Stores, Armaments, Experimental Establishments and Royal Naval Shore Establishment will be assessed to provide optimum support—at the most economical cost. 1983 will see changes in both the size and the mode of operations of the RMAS. Only when the implementation of the "run-down" policy and changes due to the events of 1982—have been itemised and effected will the future shape of the RMAS be clearly seen.

SHIPS OF THE ROYAL MARITIME AUXILIARY SERVICE — PENNANT NUMBERS

Ship	Penn. No.	Ship	Penn. No.
MELTON	A83	BEDDGELERT	A100
MENAI	A84	BEMBRIDGE	A101
MEON	A87	AIREDALE	A102
AGILE	A88	BIBURY	A103
ADVICE	A89	BLAKENEY	A104
ACCORD	A90	BRODICK	A105
MILFORD	A91		
TYPHOON	A95	ALSATIAN	A106
BEAULIEU	A99	FELICITY	A112

Ship	Penn. No.	Ship	Penn. No.
MAGNET	A114	ISABEL	A183
LODESTONE	A115	POINTER	A188
AGNES	A121	SETTER	A189
CAIRN	A126	JOAN	A190
TORRID	A127	JOYCE	A193
TORRENT	A128	GWENDOLINE	A196
DALMATIAN	A129	SEALYHAM	A197
TORNADO	A140	HELEN	A198
TORCH	A141	MYRTLE	A199
TORMENTOR	A142	SPANIEL	A201
TOREADOR	A143	NANCY	A202
DAISY	A145	NORAH	A205
WATERMAN	A146	LLANDOVERY	A207
FRANCES	A147	LAMLASH	A208
FIONA	A148	CHARLOTTE	A210
FLORENCE	A149	LECHLADE	A211
GENEVIEVE	A150	ENDEAVOUR	A213
GEORGINA	A152	BEE	A216
DEERHOUND	A155	CHRISTINE	A217
DAPHNE	A156	CLARE	A218
LOYAL HELPER	A157	LOYAL	
SUPPORTER	A158	MODERATOR	A220
LOYAL WATCHER	A159	ADEPT	A224
LOYAL VOLUNTEER	A160	BUSTLER	A225
LOYAL MEDIATOR	A161	CAPABLE	A226
ELKHOUND	A162	CAREFUL	A227
GOOSANDER	A164	CRICKET	A229
POCHARD	A165	COCKCHAFER	A230
KATHLEEN	A166	KINGARTH	A232
LABRADOR	A168	GNAT	A239
KITTY	A170	SHEEPDOG	A250
LESLEY	A172	DORIS	A252
DOROTHY	A173	LADYBIRD	A253
LILAH	A174	ST MARGARETS	A259
MARY	A175	CICALA	A263
EDITH	A177	SCARAB	A272
HUSKY	A178	ETTRICK	A274
MASTIFF	A180	ELSING	A277
IRENE	A181	KINBRACE	A281
SALUKI	A182	AURICULA	A285

Ship	Penn. No.	Ship	Penn. No.
CONFIANCE	A289	CROMARTY	A488
CONFIDENT	A290	DORNOCH	A490
ILCHESTER	A308	ROLLICKER	A502
INSTOW	A309	UPLIFTER	A507
IRONBRIDGE	A311	HEADCORN	A1766
BETTY	A322	HEVER	A1767
BRIDGET	A323	HARLECH	A1768
BRENDA	A325	HAMBLEDON	A1769
FOXHOUND	A326	LOYAL	
BASSET	A327	CHANCELLOR	A1770
COLLIE	A328	LOYAL PROCTOR	A1771
CORGI	A330	HOLMWOOD	A1772
FOTHERBY	A341	HORNING	A1773
FELSTEAD	A348	HEADCORN	A1776
CARTMEL	A350	SHIPHAM	M2726
CAWSAND	A351	PORTISHAM	M2781
ELKSTONE	A353	SANDRINGHAM	M2791
FROXFIELD	A354	MANDARIN	P192
EPWORTH	A355	PINTAIL	P193
DATCHET	A357	GARGANEY	P194
ROYSTERER	A361	GOLDENEYE	P195
DOLWEN	A362	ABINGER	Y11
DENMEAD	A363	ALNESS	Y12
WHITEHEAD	A364	ALNMOUTH	Y13
FULBECK	A365	ASHCOTT	Y16
ROBUST	A366	WATERFALL	Y17
NEWTON	A367	WATERSHED	Y18
KINTERBURY	A378	WATERSPOUT	Y19
THROSK	A379	WATERSIDE	Y20
CRICKLADE	A381	OILPRESS	Y21
APPLEBY	A383	OILSTONE	Y22
CLOVELLY	A389	OILWELL	Y23
CRICCIETH	A391	OILFIELD	Y24
GLENCOE	A392	OILBIRD	Y25
DUNSTER	A393	OILMAN	Y26
FINTRY	A394	WATERCOURSE	Y30
GRASMERE	A402	WATERFOWL	Y31
KINLOSS	A482		

RMAS Robust

ROYSTERER CLASS

Ship	Pennant Number	Completion Date	Builder
ROYSTERER	A361	1972	C.D. Holmes
ROBUST	A366	1974	C.D. Holmes
ROLLICKER	A502	1973	C.D. Holmes

G.R.T. 1036 tons **Dimensions** 54m x 12m x 6m
Speed 15 knots **Complement** 31.

Notes
Built for salvage and long range towage, but are also used for harbour duties.

77

T U G S

RMAS Typhoon

TYPHOON CLASS

Ship	Pennant Number	Completion Date	Builder
TYPHOON	A95	1960	Henry Robb

G.R.T. 1034 tons **Dimensions** 60m x 12m x 4m
Speed 17 knots **Complement** 80.

Long range towage and salvage tug. Now based at Portland and employed mainly on target towing and trails work. Served in Falklands Task Force. The older CYCLONE (A111) is for disposal at Gibraltar.

RMAS Agile

CONFIANCE CLASS

Ship	Pennant Number	Completion Date	Builder
AGILE	A88	1959	Goole SB Co.
ADVICE	A89	1959	A & J Inglis
ACCORD	A90	1958	A & J Inglis
CONFIANCE	A289	1956	A & J Inglis
CONFIDENT	A290	1956	A & J Inglis

Displacement 760 tons **Dimensions** 47m x 11m x 4m **Speed** 13 knots **Complement** 29.

Notes
Minor differences exist between the last two ships of the class. Employed in harbour, coastal towage and target towing duties. All the coastal/ocean going tugs have "bolt on" facilities for spraying oil spillages.

RMAS Adept

HARBOUR TUGS
TWIN UNIT TRACTOR TUGS (TUTT'S)

Ship	Pennant Number	Completion Date	Builder
ADEPT	A224	1980	R. Dunston
BUSTLER	A225	1981	R. Dunston
CAPABLE	A226	1981	R. Dunston
CAREFUL	A227	1982	R. Dunston

G.R.T. 375 tons	**Dimensions** 39m x 10m x 4m
Speed 12 knots	**Complement** 9

Notes
Five more of this class will be ordered in 1983 to replace the
CONFIANCE class.

DOG CLASS

Ship	Pennant Number	Ship	Pennant Number
AIREDALE	A102	POINTER	A188
ALSATIAN	A106	SETTER	A189
CAIRN	A126	SEALYHAM	A197
DALMATIAN	A129	SPANIEL	A201
DEERHOUND	A155	SHEEPDOG	A250
ELKHOUND	A162	FOXHOUND	A326
LABRADOR	A168	BASSET	A327
HUSKY	A178	COLLIE	A328
MASTIFF	A180	CORGIE	A330
SALUKI	A182		

GRT 152 tons **Dimensions** 29m x 8m x 4m **Speed** 12 knots **Complement** 8.

Notes

General harbour tugs — all completed between 1962 & 1972.

RMAS Dorothy

IMPROVED GIRL CLASS

Ship	Pennant Number	Ship	Pennant Number
DAISY	A145	CHARLOTTE	A210
DAPHNE	A156	CHRISTINE	A217
DOROTHY	A173	CLARE	A218
EDITH	A177	DORIS	A252
G.R.T. 75 tons **Speed** 10 knots **Complement** 6.			

Notes

All completed 1971-2. CLARE was serving in RN colours and with a RN crew on anti-illegal immigrant patrols in Hong Kong waters, but has now returned to harbour duties.

RMAS Kathleen

IRENE CLASS

Ship	Pennant Number	Ship	Pennant Number
KATHLEEN	A166	ISABEL	A183
KITTY	A170	JOAN	A190
LESLEY	A172	JOYCE	A193
LILAH	A174	MYRTLE	A199
MARY	A175	NANCY	A202
IRENE	A181	NORAH	A205
G.R.T. 89 tons **Speed** 8 knots **Complement** 6.			

Notes

Known as Water Tractors these craft are used for basin moves and towage of light barges.

RMAS Georgina

FELICITY CLASS

Ship	Pennant Number	Ship	Pennant Number
FELICITY	A112	GENEVIEVE	A150
FRANCES	A147	GEORGINA	A152
FIONA	A148	GWENDOLINE	A196
FLORENCE	A149	HELEN	A198
G.R.T. 80 tons **Speed** 10 knots **Complement** 6.			

Notes

Water Tractors — completed in 1973: FRANCES, FLORENCE & GENEVIEVE completed 1980.

RMAS Bridget

GIRL CLASS

Ship	Pennant Number	Ship	Pennant Number
AGNES	A121	BRIDGET	A323
BETTY	A322	BRENDA	A325
G.R.T. 38 tons **Speed** 10 knots **Complement** 6.			

Notes

Completed 1962-1972. General duties light tugs. 4 sold for commercial service in 1982. Remainder will all be sold by March 1984.

RMAS Whitehead

TRIALS SHIPS

Ship	Pennant Number	Completion Date	Builder
WHITEHEAD	A364	1971	Scotts
G.R.T. 3427 tons **Dimensions** 97m x 15m x 5m **Speed** 15.5 knots **Complement** 57.			

Notes
Fitted with Torpedo Tubes for trial firings.

RMAS Newton

Ship	Pennant Number	Completion Date	Builder
NEWTON	A367	1976	Scotts
G.R.T. 2779 tons **Dimensions** 99m x 16m x 6m **Speed** 15 knots **Complement** 64			

Notes
Built as sonar propagation trials ships but can also be used as Cable Layer.

RMAS Auricula

TEST & EXPERIMENTAL SONAR TENDER

Ship	Pennant Number	Completion Date	Builder
AURICULA	A285	1981	Ferguson Bros
G.R.T. 981 tons **Speed** 12 knots	**Dimensions** 52m x 11m x 3m **Complement** 18		

RMAS Throsk

ARMAMENT STORES CARRIERS

Ship	Pennant Number	Completion Date	Builder
KINTERBURY	A378	1980	Appledore S B
THROSK	A379	1977	Cleland SB Co.

G.R.T. 1357 tons. **Dimensions** 64m x 12m x 5m
Speed 14 knots **Complement** 22.

Notes
2 holds carry Naval armament stores, ammunition and guided missiles. Employed on short coastal journeys between Naval Bases. Kinterbury varies slightly from earlier sister ship.

RMAS Cricket

INSECT CLASS

Ship	Pennant Number	Completion Date	Builder
BEE	A216	1970	C.D. Holmes
CRICKET	A229	1972	Beverley
COCKCHAFER	A230	1971	Beverley
GNAT	A239	1972	Beverley
LADYBIRD	A253	1973	Beverley
CICALA	A263	1971	Beverley
SCARAB	A272	1973	Beverley

G.R.T. 279 tons **Dimensions** 34m x 8m x 3m **Speed** 10.5 knots **Complement** 10.

Notes
SCARAB is fitted as a Mooring Vessel and COCKCHAFER as Stores Carrier—remainder are now Naval Armament carriers.

RNXS Loyal Moderator

LOYAL CLASS

Ship	Penn No.	Ship	Penn No.
LOYAL HELPER	A157	LOYAL MEDIATOR	A161
SUPPORTER	A158	LOYAL MODERATOR	A220
LOYAL WATCHER	A159	LOYAL CHANCELLOR	A1770
LOYAL VOLUNTEER	A160	LOYAL PROCTOR	A1771

G.R.T. 112 tons **Dimensions** 24m x 6m x 3m **Speed** 10.5 knots **Complement** 6.

Notes

All these craft are operated by the Royal Naval Auxiliary Service (RNXS) — men (and women) — who in time of emergency would man these craft for duties as port control vessels. HMS ALERT and VIGILANT are similar and were taken over from the RNXS.

T
E
N
D
E
R
S

RMAS Criccieth

CLOVELLY CLASS (Type A, B & X)

Ship	Penn. No.	Ship	Penn. No.
MELTON	A83	FULBECK	A365
MENAI	A84	CRICKLADE	A381
MEON	A87	CLOVELLY	A389
MILFORD	A91	CRICCIETH	A391
LLANDOVERY	A207	GLENCOE	A392
LAMLASH	A208	DUNSTER	A393
LECHLADE	A211	FINTRY	A394
ETTRICK	A274	GRASMERE	A402
ELSING	A277	CROMARTY	A488
ILCHESTER*	A308	DORNOCH	A490
INSTOW*	A309	HEADCORN	A1766
IRONBRIDGE*	A311	HEVER	A1767
FOTHERBY	A341	HARLECH	A1768
FELSTEAD	A348	HAMBLEDON	A1769
ELKSTONE	A353	HOLMWOOD	A1772
FROXFIELD	A354	HORNING	A1773
EPWORTH	A355		
DENMEAD	A363	DATCHET	A357

G.R.T. 78 tons   **Dimensions** 24m x 6m x 3m
Speed 10.5 knots   **Complement** 6

Notes
All completed since 1971 to replace Motor Fishing Vessels. Vessels marked * are diving tenders. Remainder are Training Tenders, Passenger Ferries, or Cargo Vessels. DATCHET (A357) is a diving tender — not of this class but similar.

RMAS Beaulieu

ABERDOVEY CLASS ('63 DESIGN)

Ship	Pennant Number	Ship	Pennant Number
ABINGER	Y11	BEDDGELERT	A100
ALNESS	Y12	BEMBRIDGE	A101
ALNMOUTH	Y13	BIBURY	A103
ASHCOTT	Y16	BLAKENEY	A104
APPLEBY	A383	BRODICK	A105
BEAULIEU	A99	CARTMEL	A350
		CAWSAND	A351

G.R.T. 77 tons **Dimensions** 24m x 5m x 3m **Speed** 10.5 knots **Complement** 6.

Notes

ALNMOUTH is a Sea Cadet Training Ship based at Plymouth. BEMBRIDGE has similar duties at Portsmouth. ABERDOVEY was transferred to MOD (Army) late 1982. ABINGER attached RN Unit Aberdeen University.

RNXS Portisham

INSHORE CRAFT

Ship	Penn. No.	Ship	Penn. No.
SHIPHAM ● PORTISHAM ●	M2726 M2781	SANDRINGHAM	M2791
Displacement 164 tons **Dimensions** 32m x 6m x 2m **Speed** 12 knots **Complement** c15			

Notes

All are ex Inshore Minesweepers converted for alternative roles. Vessels marked ● are training ships for the RNXS. SANDRINGHAM is used as a Clyde ferry for service personnel.

RMAS Oilwell

OILPRESS CLASS

Ship	Pennant Number	Completion Date	Builder
OILPRESS	Y21	1969	Appledore Shipbuilders
OILSTONE	Y22	1969	" "
OILWELL	Y23	1969	" "
OIL FIELD	Y24	1969	" "
OILBIRD	Y25	1969	" "
OILMAN	Y26	1969	" "

G.R.T. 362 tons **Dimensions** 41m x 9m x 3m **Speed** 11 knots **Complement** 11.

Notes
Employed as Harbour and Coastal Oilers.

RMAS Watershed

WATER CARRIERS
WATER CLASS

Ship	Pennant Number	Completion Date	Builder
WATERCOURSE	Y15	1974	Drypool Eng. Co.
WATERFOWL	Y16	1974	Drypool Eng. Co.
WATERFALL	Y17	1967	Drypool Eng. Co.
WATERSHED	Y18	1967	Drypool Eng. Co.
WATERSPOUT	Y19	1967	Drypool Eng. Co.
WATERSIDE	Y20	1968	Drypool Eng. Co.
WATERMAN	A146	1978	Drypool Eng. Co.

G.R.T. 263 tons **Dimensions** 40m x 8m x 2m **Speed** 11 knots **Complement** 11.

Notes
Capable of coastal passages, these craft normally supply either demineralised or fresh water to the Fleet within port limits.

RMAS Lodestone

DEGAUSSING VESSELS
MAGNET CLASS

Ship	Pennant Number	Completion Date	Builder
MAGNET	A114	1979	Cleland
LODESTONE	A115	1980	Cleland
G.R.T. 828 tons **Speed** 14 knots	**Dimensions** 55m x 12m x 4m		

Notes.

LODESTONE is in Reserve but available for service at 7 days notice.

RMAS Torrid

TORPEDO RECOVERY VESSELS (TRV's)
TORRID CLASS

Ship	Pennant Number	Completion Date	Builder
TORRID	A127	1971	Cleland SB Co.
TORRENT	A128	1972	Cleland SB Co.

G.R.T. 550 tons **Dimensions** 46m x 9m x 3m **Speed** 12 knots **Complement** 17.

Notes
A stern ramps is built for the recovery of torpedoes fired for trials and exercises. A total of 32 can be carried.

RMAS Toreador

TORNADO CLASS

Ship	Pennant Number	Completion Date	Builder
TORNADO	A140	1979	Hall Russell
TORCH	A141	1980	Hall Russell
TORMENTOR	A142	1980	Hall Russell
TOREADOR	A143	1980	Hall Russell

G.R.T. 560 tons **Dimensions** 47m x 8m x 3m
Speed 14 knots **Complement** 17.

T
R
V's

RMAS St Margarets

Ship	Pennant Number	Completion Date	Builder
ST MARGARETS	A259	1944	Swan Hunter

Displacement 1,300 tons **Dimensions** 76m x 11m x 5m
Speed 12 knots

Last true cable ship in Naval service — but also employed on
trials duties. Sole survivor of triple expansion steam propulsion
in the fleet. Will be retired, without replacement, in early 1984.

RMAS Pintail

WILD DUCK CLASS

Ship	Pennant Number	Completion Date	Builder
MANDARIN	P192	1964	C. Laird
PINTAIL	P193	1964	C. Laird
GARGANEY	P194	1966	Brooke Marine
GOLDENEYE	P195	1966	Brooke Marine
GOOSANDER	A164	1973	Robb Caledon
POCHARD	A165	1973	Robb Caledon

G.R.T. 900 tons * **Dimensions** 58m x 12m x 4m
Speed 10 knots **Complement** 26.
* Vessels vary slightly.

Notes
Vessels capable of carrying out a wide range of duties laying moorings and boom defences and heavy lift salvage work. 50 tons can be lifted over the horns and 200 tons over the bow.

RMAS Uplifter

KIN CLASS

Ship	Pennant Number	Completion Date	Builder
KINGARTH	A232	1945	A. Hall Aberdeen
KINBRACE	A281	1944	A. Hall Aberdeen
KINLOSS	A482	1945	A. Hall Aberdeen
UPLIFTER	A507	1944	Smith's Dock

Displacement 1,050 tons **Dimensions** 54m x 11m x 4m **Speed** 9 knots **Complement** 34.

Notes
Coastal Salvage Vessels re-engined between 1963 & 1967. Now have same role as Wild Duck Class. LAYMOOR (P190) ex RN manned—in Reserve at Gibraltar. An order for two new Mooring/Salvage vessels can be expected in 1983 to replace two of these vessels.

RMAS Dolwen

DOLWEN CLASS

Ship	Pennant Number	Completion Date	Builder
DOLWEN (ex Hector Gulf)	A362	1962	P.K. Harris
Displacement 602 tons **Dimensions** 41m x 9m x 4m **Speed** 14 knots.			

Notes
Built as a stern trawler, then purchased for use as a Buoy tender — now used as Safety Vessel for RAE ABERPORTH (S. Wales) from her base at Pembroke Dock. ENDEAVOUR is a Torpedo Recovery/Trials Vessel at Portland.

British Aerospace V-STOL Sea Harrier FRS 1
The Sea Harrier is a maritime strike/fighter/reconnaissance aircraft now in service operating from the carriers, HMS Hermes, Invincible and Illustrious. 25 aircraft are in service with a further 14 on order.
Can carry a variety of weapons which include:- sidewinder missiles, 2″ rocket pods, bombs and 30mm Aden guns. The aircraft will eventually carry the Sea Eagle missile.

Scottish Aviation Jetstream
The 'flying classroom' for Fleet Air Arm Observers. Based at RNAS Culdrose, Cornwall. 16 in service—all in 750 squadron.
Crew 1/2 (Plus instructor and two student observers) **Length** 48′ **Height** 18′ **Wing Span** 52′ **Speed** 215 knots.

Sea King Mk 2

Westland SEA KING Mk2

Anti-submarine helicopter fitted with advance avionics including dipping sonar and radar. Armed with torpedoes and depth charges. Able to operate in all weathers and at night. Can also be used for long range Search & Rescue missions. **Crew** Four **Length** 72′ **Height** 17′ **Rotor Diameter** 62′ **Speed** 125 knots. All Mk 2 aircraft will eventually be upgraded to Mk 5 standards.

Westland SEA KING Mk5
An updated version of the Sea King Mk 2. A more sophisticated electronic package and new radome have been installed. 32 of these aircraft are now in service.

SEA KING AEW
Another modified version of the Sea King Mk2. As a result of the Falkland conflict has been fitted with an advanced airborne early warning radar which is housed in the retractable bulbous dome. Particulars as for Sea King Mk 2.

Westland LYNX

Anti-submarine attack, surface search and strike helicopter. Replacing the Wasp in small ships of the fleet. 60 delivered and a further 20 Mk 3 versions on order. Can be armed with 2 homing torpedoes, depth charges or missiles. **Crew** Two **Length** 49′ **Height** 11′ **Rotor Diameter** 42′ **Speed** 150 knots.
Powered by two Rolls Royce Gem turboshaft engines.

Westland SEA KING Mk 4 COMMANDO

A close derivative of the Sea King (ASW). Non retractable undercarriage. Able to lift underslung loads of 8,000 lbs. Can carry 27 fully equipped Royal Marines. 11 aircraft in service with 846 Naval Air Squadron. **Crew** Three **Length** 56′ **Height** 16′ **Rotor Diameter** 62′ **Speed** 140 knots.
Powered by two Rolls Royce Gnome (uprated) engines.

Westland WESSEX Mk 5
Utility helicoptor used primarily as a troop and stores carrier in support of Royal Marine Commando's. Also used in S.A.R. Role at Culdrose, Portland and Lee-on-Solent. **Crew** 1/2 pilots + aircrewman. 59 are in service, 4 in storage and 8 undergoing modernisation.
Length 65′ **Height** 16′ **Rotor Diameter** 65′ **Speed** 115 knots. Powered by two Rolls Royce Bristol Gnome engines.

Westland WASP (HMS Endurance Flight)

Anti-submarine and F.P.B. helicoptor carried by frigates. Armed with 2 torpedoes or missiles. Also carried for general duties in H Class Survey Ships and HMS ENDURANCE (under review). Being replaced by the Lynx, but are expected to remain in service (in small numbers) until 1992.

Crew 1/2 **Length** 40' **Height** 11' **Rotor Diameter** 32' **Speed** 110 knots.

Powered by one Rolls Royce Nimbus turboshaft engine.

Westland WESSEX Mk 3

Anti-submarine aircraft carried by County Class Destroyers—predecessor to the Sea King. The large "hump" behind the rotor head houses the surface/search radar. Few aircraft remain and all will retire shortly.

Details as for the Wessex Mk 5. **Crew** 2 pilots, observer and aircrewman.

Westland/Aerospatiale GAZELLE
Basic Helicoptor Trainer for the Royal Navy and used operationally by the Royal Marines. 29 in service with the Fleet Air Arm at RNAS Culdrose. **Crew** one **Length** 39′ **Height** 10′ **Rotor Diameter** 34′ **Speed** 167 knots.
Powered by one Turbomeca Astazon 111A turboshaft engine.

Communications Aircraft

RNAS Yeovilton operate 4 Sea Herons and RNAS Culdrose operate 2 Sea Devons for Fishery Protection and General Communications Duties. 2 further Sea Devons are for sale.

Sea Heron C Mk 1 [top]
Crew 2/3 **Length** 48′ **Height** 16′ **Wing Span** 71′ **Speed** 182 knots.
Powered by 4 Gypsy Queen Air Cooled engines.

Sea Devon C Mk 20 [bottom]
Crew 2 **Length** 39′ **Height** 13′ **Wing Span** 57′ **Speed** 205 knots.
Powered by 2 Gypsy Queen Air cooled engines.

At the end of the line . . .

Readers may well find other warships afloat which are not mentioned in this book. The majority have fulfilled a long and useful life and are now relegated to non-seagoing duties. The following list gives details of their current duties:

Penn. No.	Ship	Remarks
A134	RAME HEAD	Maintenance Ship. Used as an Accommodation Ship at Portsmouth
A191	BERRY HEAD	As above, but at Devonport
C35	BELFAST	World War II Cruiser On permanent display — Pool of London.
D73	CAVALIER	World War II Destroyer. Museum Ship at Southampton. (Open to the public)
F32	SALISBURY	Cathedral Class Frigate Harbour Training and Accommodation Ship at Devonport.
F48 & F54	DUNDAS & HARDY	Captain Class Frigates Accommodation Ships at Portsmouth.
F73 & F80	EASTBOURNE & DUNCAN	Type 12 & Captain Class Frigates — Both Engineers Harbour Training Ships at Rosyth.
F97 & F117	RUSSELL & ASHANTI	Captain & Tribal Class Frigates — Engineers Harbour Training Ships at Gosport
S05	FINWHALE	Porpoise Class Submarine Harbour Training Ship at Gosport.
S67	ALLIANCE	Submarine Museum Ship at Gosport. (Open to the public)

At the time of publishing the following ships were awaiting tow for scrap or sale.

PORTSMOUTH	PLYMOUTH	CHATHAM	ROSYTH
Tiger (C20)	Forth (A187)	Dreadnought (S101)	Brighton (F106)
Devonshire (DO2)	Narwhal (S03)	Mohawk (F125)	
Palliser (F94)	Aveley (M2002)	Eskimo (F119)	
Grenville (F197)	Flintham (M2628)		
Bulwark (RO8)	Dittisham (M2621)		
Porpoise (SO1)	Dee (P3104)		